WHAT PEOPLE ARE SAYING ABOUT *TRENDING UP* . . .

"Roma and I have seen firsthand the power that social media has to build community, raise awareness, and ignite viral passion around important topics. In *Trending Up*, you will hear from some of the leading social media experts in today's church. From our first meeting in 2013, I have been inspired by their commitment to come together across denominational lines to strengthen the voice of the church in today's culture. These are active practitioners who have their finger on the pulse of the rapidly changing world of social media communications."

— *Mark Burnett, TV producer*

"More than anything else, our nation needs churches that take seriously the call to prayer, and spreading the gospel. We need an awakening from God. He can do more in a moment than we can do in a lifetime.

In the years of 2014-2016 I served as the president of the Southern Baptist Convention. The charge for the next Great Awakening in America was my charge to those within my denomination and many other church leaders across denominational lines.

I'm grateful for the leading helping churches share the tive ways online. There is a

a great work for Christ can be done there. I pray that more and more churches will take advantage of this moment of opportunity to share Christ online and that we see God move in amazing ways."

— *Dr. Ronnie Floyd, senior pastor, Cross Church; former president of the Southern Baptist Convention*

"At NRB, we have a legacy of networking and equipping religious organizations to tell that life-changing story through any variety of means. In this book you'll find a diverse collection of church communications specialists responding to the questions that all churches face on social media. *Trending Up* isn't technical drivel that is difficult to understand and quickly irrelevant. Instead, each writer stays focused on the underlying principles of social media communication, which are timeless. *Trending Up* is a must-read for any church or ministry staff!"

— *Jerry A. Johnson, PhD, president and CEO, National Religious Broadcasters*

"*Trending Up* is chock-full of practical social media advice that will benefit a church of any size. It breaks down complex social media themes and offers simple techniques to create powerful content that will uplift, inspire, and point people to God's amazing story of unwavering grace. Every church has a story that can change the course of people's lives. Surely there are moments during its worship experiences and events that would benefit others beyond its live audiences. Social media is the perfect space to extend the reach of these moments and enable them to impact a wider viewership.

I unreservedly recommend *Trending Up* to anyone who wants to better leverage social media to make an impact for God's kingdom."

— *Kyle Michael Miller, former digital producer for TODAY Show*

"This book is a must-read for anyone who is looking to improve their church social media. Read this book and learn from the best."

— *Jason Romano, former ESPN producer, host of the Sports Spectrum Podcast*

"For many people, social media presents the first and final interactions they have each day. It opens the doors to new relationships, reconnects those who have grown apart, and allows ideas to spread rapidly. Just as early believers took full advantage of the Pax Romana to further the gospel to the ends of their known world, we, too, have a unique opportunity to reach the billions of active users on social media with the gospel. Is your church prepared?

In *Trending Up*, this group of communicators from various denominations and organizations take their knowledge and experience of the ever-changing landscape of social media and boil it down to practical concepts from which your church can benefit. As you read, ask yourself how your church—as well as your personal social media platforms—can present Christ clearly to a culture that needs Him desperately."

— *Dr. George O. Wood, general superintendent, General Council of the Assemblies of God*

"As an illusionist, I have had the opportunity to travel across the world, not only to entertain audiences but to talk with them about what matters most. In recent years, I have had the privilege to direct STORY, which is a unique tribe of storytellers from organizations both inside and outside the church. The community at STORY has come to understand deeply that great stories are what change the world.

Trending Up gets me dreaming of what could happen if faith communities everywhere were taught to tell better stories—all pointing to the gospel. Many of my friends have featured their collective wisdom in this great book, and I dream it will inspire a new generation of creators, storytellers, and artists on behalf of the church."

— *Harris III, storyteller, illusionist, and director of STORY Conference*

TRENDING UP

Social Media Strategies for Today's Church

Mark Forrester
General Editor

SALUBRIS®
RESOURCES

NOTE: Some of the names in this book, as well as some identifying
details, have been changed to protect the anonymity of the people
involved.

ISBN: 978-1-68067-184-1

Printed in the United States of America

20 19 18 17 • 1 2 3 4 5

CONTENTS

FOREWORD

On a hot summer day in Nashville, I found myself talking to a group of social media directors from organizations representing much of American Christianity. Although there were only about forty people in the room, the event trended on Twitter for the next seventeen hours. This collection of young influencers were doing something remarkable—something most of us assume never happens.

They were gathering across denominational lines—what some might even consider "competitive" lines—to focus on one thing: what can we learn from each other?

Lutherans with Baptists. Pentecostals with Methodists. Conservatives with liberals . . . coming together because they knew they would all grow that way. In that gathering—in that same collaborative air—this book was set in motion.

It wasn't long into leading a dynamic movement of young leaders at Catalyst that I saw some remarkable recurring trends in leaders who could rise above the normal and get things done. Those simple but transformative principles led me to write both *The Catalyst Leader* and *H3 Leadership*, driving home the concepts of be humble, stay hungry, always hustle.

Chief among the habits of H3 is the powerful action of collaboration: simply working together to accomplish a vision and mission bigger than any of us can accomplish on our own. Among leaders in the church today, we need more collaboration and less competition. We need leaders who celebrate the victories of others, and not just their own. We need leaders with humility, combined with confidence. We need leaders with a high level of passion and skill who never settle and never stop growing. We need leaders who realize it's not about them; it's about making a difference for those they lead.

The next generation expects to find you beside them in the trenches, not in the corner office sipping espresso—humble, hungry, and hustling, not arrogant and entitled. Beside your team, not out in front of them.

In this ground-breaking book, you sit at the feet of some of the best young leaders in church communication and social media. They are pioneers and practitioners, wrestling with how to raise the bar for multiplying and amplifying the message of thousands of churches across a number of mediums and outlets. This book will uncover answers to important church communication questions, along with supercharging your church's reach and impact. In the spirit of the group, don't simply gloss over it. Bring your team together around the ideas and pass them on to other churches in your city. Let's see what we can all do together.

— *Brad Lomenick, former president of Catalyst;*
   author, H3 Leadership *and* The Catalyst Leader

FOREWORD

SPIRITUAL AWAKENINGS ARE NO SMALL THINGS, PARTICU-LARLY when God picks a mountain lodge aptly named Sleeping Lady. There I was, five years ago, up early to make the most of my first day of a writing retreat. My goals were bold: add five thousand words to my stalled-out novel; finish a speech for a C-suite level executive; write myself a new keynote speech on the power of story . . . all in two days. (You have permission to laugh. God certainly did.)

Alone in the cafeteria, I had commandeered the largest table. Maximum square footage was necessary, considering my supplies:

Prayer journal: check.

Bible, the massive amount of homework that is Bible Study Fellowship, and two devotionals: check.

A stack of research books for various speeches: check.

I was the librarian-in-chief of my own little library. The problem, of course, was that I am supposed to be a creator of stories, not just a curator of one.

As I always do, I began the day with my prayer journal, which might possibly be better named the "pity-me journal," as in, *Oh, Lord, I'm stuck on this novel. Why did I choose such a hard story to write? I'm never, ever going to finish it.* In the midst of my third or fourth paragraph bemoaning my soon-to-be-fate as a has-been writer, God spoke. And He was clear.

All stories are opportunities to tell the Truth.

Let me just say that I snapped awake in a sleeping-lady-meets-speaking-Lord way. Prayers flew out of my head and onto the page, spurred by this startling call: Stop whining. Start writing because as storytellers, we are on a divine mission. Stories are the way to create change, share meaning, and connect with others. Stories inspire and galvanize. Stories awaken.

This includes stories of all forms, from the very old to the very new—sermons and speeches, parables and novels, hymns and hip-hop, posts on church doors and Facebook walls.

That makes sense. Neuroscience research shows that the way many people learn and remember information is through story. No wonder God is the Master Storyteller, Jesus is the Living Word, and the Holy Spirit nudges us to be the plot twist in our lives—and others'.

It was as if I took dictation that morning: I captured those thoughts in what became my keynote, "The Power of Storytelling in Your Speech."

Not long afterwards, I gave that speech at a social media conference hosted at Walt Disney World, and there I met Mark Forrester, the talented director of public relations and communications for the General Council of the Assemblies of God. It was a divine appointment. A year later, Mark invited me to speak at The Best of Social Media Summit at Saddleback Church. Five minutes into the summit, I was flooded with a feeling of homecoming: These are my people—storytellers who tell stories to illuminate the Truth! Many of those same social media experts are the contributors to this book, and it's a veritable gift to all of us that they are generously sharing their expertise in how we can harness social media to share the love of God.

Here's what I learned from these social media mavens—and what makes me so happy that so many more storytellers can share in their collective wisdom. As storytellers, we write for an audience of One, but the power of a story is in its sharing. A story gains momentum in its retelling. That's the Gutenberg principle, after all. The first printing press, as contributor Todd Adkins aptly points out in chapter 1, enabled the wider-spread circulation of the Bible. Social media is our twenty-first century

Gutenberg with the ability to spread the Word farther and faster than ever before.

The power and beauty of social media is that now we can reach globally and relate individually. We can—with a single tweet or post—amplify, unify, and glorify. Social media is, as contributor Brian Orme points out, positioning ourselves in the midst of the one billion people on Facebook, and the one hundred million on Instagram, and whatever new social media outlet becomes the next, next thing. Using these tools, we now have the power to engage—truly engage—with people around the world. We can be a force of love in today's global conversations. Social media is our tool of mass encouragement in times of both global and personal despair.

Trending Up will teach you how to employ the power and beauty of social media. It's your go-to guide to all things social media today. From strategy to tactics, you'll learn to create a unique plan that perfectly aligns to your goals for your particular church or ministry. Step-by-step, this guide will give you the confidence to explore and experiment with new ways to engage with people, turning them from congregants to community to church.

As for me, personally? I love how this book inspires, challenges, and beckons all storytellers to awaken to our call of sharing the Truth and His love.

— *Justina Chen, author of* The Art of Inspiration

INTRODUCTION

"WE NEED THIS!"

I said these words at the end of lunch at a multichurch conference in 2012. The leaders of the Church of God and the Assemblies of God had met for a quick meal, and a few others of us had tagged along.

The lunch conversation was full of hope. We shared stories of amazing things we had seen God do through social media. We also talked about upcoming initiatives in our movement and how social media could play a part in those.

I bummed a ride back to Atlanta's Gwinnett Arena with the brilliant and entrepreneurial Clark Campbell, who at the time led social media efforts for the Church of God. It was then that we knew we needed a space for dialogue like that to happen across denominational lines on a regular basis.

The next day, I met Matt Brown, a young evangelist whose huge following on social media has provided him endless opportunities to share the gospel. I told Matt about the conversations of the previous day. Within hours, he had called in some connections, and we started a small, private, peer-to-peer group to allow social media directors for leading Christian denominations, organizations, and churches to collaborate on effective social media strategy. The thought was that together, we could raise the bar for Christian communications on social media.

As the years have gone by, this group has become like family. Almost daily, we're helping each other through difficult situations, sharing ideas, or even analyzing failures. One thing we all have in common—we all regularly receive questions from churches about social media. Many times, we'll draft a message to a friend in our group to help us find the right answer for the church or pastor who is asking.

That's what leads us here.

Social media is the Wild West of communications and marketing. Every day, it seems a new social-media platform, tool, or service pops up and causes us all to go back to the drawing board. In the midst of all of that chaos, a 2013 report by *Advertising Age* indicated that there were more than 181,000 self-proclaimed social media gurus, masters, mavens, or ninjas. Just think of all of those voices scrambling to make sense of the daily shifts and struggles in the social media landscape!

This book serves as more than just another list of best guesses from self-proclaimed gurus. Rather, it's a compilation of questions we frequently receive from a variety of churches. We passed each question through our panel of practitioners and assigned it to a professional with exceptional experience in that area to answer.

As communicators of God's truth, we're part of an ancient guild of men and women who have vividly painted pictures of Christ with powerful words through the ages. As these words have moved from voice to paper to screen, they still have power to communicate the life-changing message of Christ. It's a responsibility and calling that the contributors to this book hold dear.

In *Trending Up*, you'll find the collective wisdom of many thought leaders in the social media sphere. In addition to answering questions, they have also contributed to a Resources Appendix, offering their suggestions for books, websites, blogs, platforms, and tools to help you dive in, or dive in more deeply. More than anything, however, you'll find a passion from these leaders to equip you with the practical knowledge and helpful insights you need to connect with your church and reach your community.

And to that, we can collectively say, "We need this!"

— *Mark Forrester, director of public relations and communications, General Council of the Assemblies of God*

Chapter 1
Why Social Media?

YEARS AGO, I REMEMBER VISITING THE NATION OF ENGLAND'S website after I heard that the engagement of Prince William and Kate Middleton had been announced on Twitter. The website's front-and-center call to action was to become a fan of England's Facebook page.

In 2011, some 3,400 miles away in the Middle East, Facebook reportedly played a key role in stirring up the 2011 revolution and subsequent overthrow of the government in Egypt. When the government there shut down Facebook to keep people from exposing its atrocities, people took to the streets for weeks until the government and its leaders were toppled. Facebook has been so influential in giving people a voice and mobilizing protests that people in the Middle East have even named their children Facebook! Don't believe me? Check it out at www.dailymail. co.uk/news/article-1358876. In America, headlines often break on Twitter before the major news outlets can announce them.

Social media has not only changed our daily routine, relationships, and the way we relate to the world, it has also, quite literally, changed our world.

So when we ask, "Why social media?" we have to first realize the powerful force it has become and then ask, "How can the church leverage this power for the gospel?" How can we take the most creative and dynamic innovation of the twenty-first century and use this technology to tell the greatest story ever told in fresh new ways?

Social media offers tools to share your church's news, but more importantly it gives you the potential to reach hundreds or even thousands of people who may never step foot inside the doors of your church. Not only is social media a mind-boggling opportunity, I and my friends who share in this book believe it is a sacred responsibility: "From everyone who has been given much, much will be demanded" (Luke 12:48).

In this chapter, we'll ask and answer some questions to help you make decisions about how (or if) your church will engage in social media by exploring its impact on the church and communication thus far. Here's a quick overview of the questions we'll answer:

- Has social media been destructive or constructive for the church? (Todd Adkins)

- How is social media changing the way we communicate in our churches? (Brian Orme)

- Should my church be on social media? (David Drury)

—Matt Brown

HAS SOCIAL MEDIA BEEN DESTRUCTIVE OR CONSTRUCTIVE FOR THE CHURCH?

Todd Adkins, director of the Leadership Division, LifeWay Christian Resources

In the fifteenth century, Johannes Gutenberg invented a new technology that introduced the era of "mass communication" and ushered in a complete restructure of the society of the day. The printing press disrupted everything. For the first time, the circulation of information and ideas could move unrestricted across the boundaries of geography and social class. Within a decade, this free flow of information rapidly changed socioeconomics, religion, and cultures, not to mention toppling a few governments and institutions along the way.

Does this sound familiar?

Prior to the printing press, books were expensive and primarily owned by churches and educational institutions as nearly every book was painstakingly produced by hand. The creation of a book could take years—a process primarily reserved for scribes who lived in monasteries with a special room called a scriptorium. Books were considered precious objects containing special knowledge that was guarded by the church and educational institutions. If you wanted to get this special knowledge, you needed to show up when the doors were open.

Does this sound familiar?

It just so happened that the invention of the printing press occurred around the same time a radical cleric named Martin Luther penned his Ninety-five Theses railing against the established church. Thanks to the printing press, his writings could now be widely distributed, leading to a little thing we call the Reformation. Don't miss the fact that the printing press used to print indulgences was the same one used to print Luther's broadsheets opposing indulgences, which ultimately ushered in the Reformation. Was the invention of the printing press good or evil? The answer, of course, is neither. We should never confuse the medium with the message.

You might wonder if social media has been destructive for the contemporary church because of stories you've heard. You may be asking: Isn't social media just full of garbage and the worst parts of our society? The reality is that Christ called us to be salt and light, going into all of the world to meet people where they are and to share the gospel message of Jesus Christ.

Today, we face a stark reality that "where they are" is on their smartphones. According to the most recent Total Audience Report[1] from Neilson, well over 80 percent of consumers use smartphones, and those smartphone users are checking their phones almost 150 times a day! What are they checking the first thing in the morning, the last thing at night, between lunch breaks, bathroom breaks, and commercial breaks? Social media.

When the apostle Paul came to a new place, he immediately went to wherever the people were: the town square, the synagogues, the local Mars Hill. Consider his words in his first letter to the church of Corinth: "To the weak I became weak, to win the weak. I have become all things to all people, so that by all possible means I might save some. I do all of this for the sake of the gospel, that I may share in its blessings" (1 Corinthians 9:22–23).

As someone who's passionate about developing leaders and equipping the church to be the church, I see a huge need for engaging the culture where it is today. We must raise the cross once again at the center of the conversation, wherever that may be. Is it safe and constructive to engage in social media? Is it a clean environment? Can I fully control it? No, actually it's sometimes extremely destructive, dark with porn, gambling, and other unpleasant things. However, let's remember that the gospel wasn't manifested in Pleasantville or Mayberry. Our Lord and Savior was hung on a tree between cursing thieves by men who mocked Him and gambled for His clothes. He gave His life in that kind of place for that kind of people.

Ultimately, Jesus and His followers were about reaching people—and people are what today's church should be about as well.

ᑎ   ᑎ   ᑎ   ᑎ

HOW HAS SOCIAL MEDIA CHANGED COMMUNICATION?

Brian Orme, content director, Outreach, Inc.

"What are you doing?" I asked my teenage son, Noah, in the car on the way to school. He was fidgeting with his phone, and it looked like he was hiding something.

"Nothing, Dad," he said.

I put on my parenting face and asked, again. "Noah, tell me what you're doing, right now! Who are you Snapchatting?"

"All right! Sometimes I send a verse to my friends in the morning to encourage them; that's all."

"Oh, uh . . . carry on."

As a parent, this was one of those cool, "we-did-something-right" moments. My teenage son was using social media to lift up others with the life-giving words of Scripture. A small parenting win! It's also a poignant example of the way social media has changed the communication game.

As the content director at Outreach, Inc., I oversee numerous websites and social media communities. Through Facebook, our primary publishing platform, we share stories and build relationships with millions of people across the world. We see men and women give their lives to Christ, recommit to their marriages, decide to adopt or foster kids, and engage important issues like ending extreme global poverty or sex trafficking—all through the vehicle of social media. It's humbling and inspiring at the same time.

Yet, social media is often messy, too. The conversations don't always go as planned. Sometimes readers misunderstand our intent. Sometimes we do a poor job of communicating, and other times people are just, well, mean. Just like real life.

Social media is far from a communication utopia, but it's radically changing the way we communicate with each other. How, exactly, is the rise of social media platforms like Twitter, Facebook, Instagram, Snapchat, and Periscope changing the way we connect and communicate in our churches? Glad you asked.

- Social media is amplifying our voice to reach more people than ever before in history.

Just as the printing press revolutionized the way people communicated in culture-shifting ways, social media is expanding our reach today on a scale like no other in history.

Marshall McLuhan, writer, professor, and philosopher of communication theory, believed all technology is an extension of the human body: Wheels are an extension of the feet; radio an extension of voice; the printing press, the hands; guns, the fist.[2] I agree with McLuhan, and I would suggest social media is an extension of both voice and community. The potential for the church to amplify the most important message in history through social media is epic. Think about this: One billion people are active on Facebook, and one hundred million people use Instagram every month. Tom Webster, vice president of strategy at Edison Research, says 54 percent of all Americans have a profile on a social media site, and 23 percent of Facebook users check their account five or more times a day.[3]

Today, you have the opportunity to extend the gospel to more people than your physical ministry could ever do on its own. Why not leverage this tool to amplify the message of Christ—reaching out to the farthest corners of the world to extend the truth, mission, and love of God?

In his book, *Flickering Pixels*, Shane Hipps writes, "Christianity is fundamentally a communication event. . . . God wants to communicate with us, and His media are many: angels, burning bushes, stone tablets, scrolls, donkeys, prophets, mighty voices, still whispers, and shapes traced in the dirt."[4]

If God used donkeys and dirt to communicate, I'm confident He can use social media.

Tip: Find out where the majority of the people in your church are already engaged on social media and begin there. Start with one platform relevant to your church and do it well. Don't overload your church with every available social media platform

- Social media is accelerating the speed at which we communicate.

Early in world history, it took years for news to travel across the globe. Through technology, that gap was shortened to months, then days, then hours, and now it only takes a nanosecond. Today, disasters, world events, uprisings, and downfalls are relayed around the globe through Twitter, Facebook, and Periscope in real time. We can reach more people and reach them faster than ever before in history.

Tip: Using social media is not just about transferring information, but cultivating relational equity. Don't look at it as another church program—or an extension of your weekly bulletin. Instead, invest in your people, listen to them, and learn to share amazing stories together.

• Social media is changing the way we see the world.

According to the Pew Research Center, about 71 percent of eighteen- to twenty-nine-year-olds cite the Internet as their central news source.[5] We're no longer waiting for local or national news broadcasts to tell us what's happening in the world today. Instead, we're using our mobile phones and social media. And, in doing this, social media platforms like Facebook are shaping the algorithms based on our behaviors—letting us select the most important stories in the world today through our clicks and engagement. The result? Social media is becoming the psychological stomping grounds for human beings to express what they love, hate, fear, and cherish.

We're standing at such a unique time in history. In the coming years, we'll see the impact of social media like never before, and if we use this tool wisely, our work for the gospel could hit a tipping point that changes history, once again, for the kingdom.

I hope your church will be a part of it.

SHOULD MY CHURCH BE ON SOCIAL MEDIA?

David Drury, chief of staff, The Wesleyan Church

Whether you lead a church or an organization that serves the church, ministry is complicated with cultural challenges our grandparents could never have seen coming. So why should we pay attention to social media in the middle of all this change?

I get it. I've been there. I've been a founding pastor of a small church plant where my cell phone was the only "church phone." I've been in the middle of church fights and conflicts. Apparently, so have most church leaders. In a recent survey of U.S. pastors, 84 percent said they are "on call twenty-four hours a day." Some 80 percent say they "expect conflict in their church" on a routine basis, more than half find their role "frequently overwhelming," and almost half feel "the demands of ministry are more than they can handle."[6]

So, perhaps you think we should just tune all this out, unplug, and make ministry more "authentic" and much less chaotic. You may have concerns about bullying or privacy. Perhaps you think social media is a huge waste of productivity, and everyone is using it to goof off way too much.

Okay, yes, we probably are all goofing off too much. But can we dismiss social media that easily? As you consider whether or not to dive in or dive more deeply and how your church should pursue social media opportunities, I want to give you some thoughts on ministry in a social media world.

• Social media can correct individualistic consumerism.

When I sit with my kids at the dinner table, I sometimes ask them these questions: "What did you learn today? What did you consume today? What did you create today?" The answer to the first question usually happens at school, the second on television (or more often for kids today, on YouTube.) Creating is harder to come by.

Whether someone is sharing a picture of her cat or a personal testimony video about reading the Bible, social media can be a powerful way to actually create things and share them with others, beyond isolated consuming,

At the same time, as ministry leaders we need to set personal boundaries to keep us from converting social media into negative consumption. Likewise, we don't want to enter social media spaces in a divisive, angry, or petty way, further isolating others from us, the church and, ultimately, Jesus.

- Social media is a "calling."

My grandpa was a minister in the coal-mining hills of Pennsylvania. I still have the little booklet where he tracked every "call" he made to someone's house to eat pie and hopefully talk about spiritual things. He would track his "callings" with a list of hash-mark-style ticks in his book.

Today, pastors can track their progress through social media hashtags, not hash marks. I know a pastor who checks her Facebook page twice a day to discover the needs in her congregation so that she can respond appropriately.

My grandpa showed up for "pie with the pastor" in part because it was expected. Today, in the world of social media, when someone posts about a death in their family on Facebook, they expect ministry leaders to show up in the comments section.

- Your absence on social media is noted.

A recent survey shows that two-thirds of American adults now use social media (up from just 7 percent a decade ago), and nine out of ten young adults ages eighteen to twenty-nine are using social media. Even latecomers to the social media party (those sixty-five and older) have still tripled over the last five years.[7] Your people are already on social media, and if you are not, your absence has been noted.

The various, ever-changing social media platforms provide the opportunity for us to intentionally influence the conversation. Just as Paul went to Mars Hill in Acts 17, we can show up where the public conversation is currently taking place. And as my friend Todd Adkins pointed out at the beginning of this chapter, today those conversations are on social media.

• They're already talking about your church.

Newcomers to a church used to call or drive by the building before visiting. As technology developed, they would probably check out the church's website. Now? People check out what people are saying about your church on social media before they visit your church or your website.

Ministry in a social media world starts simply: Just pay attention. Set up one or two social media accounts and schedule time to pay attention, encouraging the best in your people and reaching out to new people. You want to pay attention because social media is the new town square of every community and the water cooler conversation of every ministry.

A Case Study

Social Media in Action

How One Church Is Connecting to Potential Visitors

The leaders of Waterline Church in the Indianapolis suburb of Fishers, Indiana, found that the first place people were finding them was on social media.

"They skip our great website and instead find our people instantly on Facebook so they see what we're doing and saying today," says John Freed, founding pastor of the growing five-year-old church. Freed doesn't mind this reality at all.

"It allows for people to connect with the unique culture of our church, instead of the more polished website," he says. Waterline gets "referral credibility"—something they know they'll never get from a mailer or a website.

The church has found that social media offers a new language, allowing for easy participation. Eventually, Waterline decided to use social media as a primary communication tool, in part, Freed says, because (1) it's free and (2) it isn't difficult.

At the same time, he has some reservations. Social media is such a fluid environment, the "rules" are always changing.

"While you can create a presence on several social media outlets, focusing most of your energy on just one platform and owning it is best," he cautions, adding that managing too many platforms and keeping up with all the new developments for each one will likely leave you spread too thin and feeling overwhelmed. Privacy is also a concern for Freed, who treats his own personal social media use as entirely public. "I don't say or show something on Facebook that I wouldn't also say or show from the stage."

What's more, Freed warns against misuse by pastors who use social media for private and personal means. Instead, he casts a vision for social media as a useful ministry tool, if wielded properly. "You must make sure it isn't disruptive or distracting to your ministry. Social media should help, not hurt."

— *D. D.*

Chapter 2
Content Strategy

CAN YOU IMAGINE READING A STORY THAT'S MISSING THE plot?

Sounds crazy, right? The plot is crucial to the success and quality of a story. It connects the dots from one point to the other. Put simply, a story without a plot is just a huge waste of time and energy. In the same way, a content strategy is as important to your social media efforts as a plot is to any story. The content strategy provides the "why" behind every post, image, story, and event you share.

Taking the time to develop a strategy provides a road map for you and your church, while bringing clarity and focus as you connect with people online. By setting up and framing your followers' expectations, you strengthen your church brand and more cohesively align your voice with your church's vision and mission. Plus, a content strategy allows volunteers on your team to connect with and think about the big picture when sharing or posting on social media. And a solid strategy takes the pressure off when filtering what or what not to post. When your strategy is attached to a vision, you'll know specifically what you're targeting and if, or when, you hit your targets. Most importantly, when you take the time to develop a strong strategy, you give people a reason to follow you on social media and share your content. People naturally feel led to connect and engage with you.

As God's Plan A for the world, the church needs to share its stories with more people. Developing a content strategy sets you firmly on the path to accomplishing that. Throughout this chapter, social media experts will share their insights and experience, answering three crucial content strategy questions:

- How do I determine my goals for social media? (Drew Gneiser)

- What should I post based on my social media goals? (Chad Cannon)

- What makes content "sticky"? (Matt Brown)

—Haley Veturis

HOW DO I DETERMINE MY GOALS FOR SOCIAL MEDIA?

Drew Gneiser, social media specialist

I've seen it happen dozens of times.

You're sitting in front of a computer screen, staring at it, with no idea what to post. It used to be so easy! You had tons of ideas and excitement, but now it's as though someone turned off the faucet. Pretty soon you wonder if you have an ounce of creativity or why your church should bother with social media at all. Sometimes this moment even happens when your Facebook page is just three weeks old.

It doesn't have to be this way. You can avoid hitting unnecessary and frustrating roadblocks by creating social media goals.

• Getting to Where You Want to Go

Preparation for a marathon and preparation for sumo wrestling look very different. The runner and wrestler will both focus on stamina, quickness, mental toughness, and body weight, but each will prepare in distinctive ways designed to reach their specific goals.

In the same way, before you can talk about your church's social media goals, you need to understand the church's ministry goals. Without clear goals and strategy, you could become a marathon runner trying desperately to survive in a sumo ring. Having clear, defined ministry goals helps you outline a social media content strategy and then provides a blueprint of sorts to show you how to get where you want to go.

Clarified goals can also help prevent personal arguments. If you haven't already, you'll soon learn that many people on your staff or team will have their own ideas about what, how, and when to post to your church's social media platforms. Unfortunately, most of these ideas won't necessarily correspond to your church's overall vision. Instead of talking about whether or not an idea is "good" or "bad," evaluate whether or not the idea fits with your church's ministry goals and strategy. Goals can diffuse potentially hurtful disagreements and unify teams around a common direction. As someone who has created and executed social media content strategies for churches and companies, I've seen firsthand the value of setting overarching goals.

• Setting Goals: Four Things to Consider

Before you set your social media goals, consider your church's vision and mission and how your goals might support a content strategy.

1. **Identify your church's unique purpose.** When people think about your church, what comes to mind? Does your church have a heart for the homeless? Single moms? Family ministry? A passion for deep prayer? Global justice? Worship through the arts? Find that one thing in your DNA that makes your church special and unique and lean into it.

    If your church's vision or mission is to minister to families, for example, then your social media goals should include ministering to families. This is so important! Remember that social media goals should be anchored to your church's ministry goals.

2. **Preach the gospel.** This may seem obvious, but it's worth saying. All churches should exist to preach the gospel, so your social media goals should reflect this truth. How is "sharing the gospel" reflected in your

social media goals? Can you concretely point to evidence that you're accomplishing this goal?

3. **Deepen relationships inside your church.** Relationships are made, exist, and grow in many ways. Sometimes we have coffee with a friend. Sometimes we talk on the phone. We may worship in a sanctuary together or read each other's Facebook statuses.

   One of your major social media goals should be to deepen relationships among the members of your church. How does (or will) your church leverage social media to foster encouragement, increase participation, start deeper conversations, and lift up prayer among members? Do your social media goals reflect this kind of interaction?

4. **Draw new people to church.** This was mentioned in chapter 1, but it bears repeating. Before visiting your church for the first time, many people will visit your website or social media pages. Your social media goals should include how you will invite and welcome new people to your church.

   For example, can someone tweet your church to ask about service times and quickly get a response (within a few hours)? Make it a goal to respond to everyone who interacts with your church.

- Setting SMART Goals

One popular list of criteria for setting and evaluating any goal is the acronym SMART: specific, measurable, attainable, relevant, and timely. Here's how this method might look for social media.

1. **Specific.** What do you want this goal to accomplish? Will this goal draw more people to your church? Offer encouragement? Bring awareness to a key ministry? Remember to connect the social media goal to your church's vision and mission. *Ask:* What are our specific outcomes for this social media goal?

2. **Measurable.** How much and when? A measurable goal could include the number of times people share your post, new followers, views, and number of clicks. (Note: The number of followers doesn't reflect the whole picture and shouldn't be your only goal. People can—and do—buy fake followers to make their numbers look better.) Your goal should reflect the importance of drawing the right people, not just more people, as well as cultivating engagement and partici-pation. *Ask:* Is this goal measurable? If so, what are our metrics for knowing we accomplished it?

3. **Attainable.** You probably won't get (and don't need) a million views, so aim for a goal you can reach. Then celebrate! If last week you had four people share posts from your Facebook page, your next goal could be five shares (but not one hundred). *Ask:* Can we realistically reach this goal?

4. **Relevant.** Social media gives you the tools you need to accomplish many different things. Remember that not all of them matter. Will this social media goal contrib-ute to your church's goals? Is this the right time for the goal? Each week, focus on the most pertinent things. *Ask:* How does this goal connect to our church's goals at this point in time?

5. **Timely.** Give yourself a deadline: "In the next two

weeks/one month/one year, we will _____." A deadline gives you a timeframe to measure against future goals. It also keeps your team accountable for reaching the goals. *Ask:* What is our deadline for hitting this goal?

It's time to get to work. As soon as possible, put something, anything, on paper. Your social media goals don't need to be perfect. Make sure you involve your team (never set goals in a vacuum), continuing to ask, how do these goals align with our church's vision and mission?

ᴒ   ᴒ   ᴒ   ᴒ

WHAT SHOULD I POST, BASED ON MY GOALS?

Chad Cannon, chief marketing officer for Michael Hyatt & Co.

I love this question. I always say, "Goals are first." Never proceed with any marketing initiatives (no matter how creative or proven they are) without first stating your goals. Once you identify and finalize your social media goals, though, there are practical strategies for how to meet them through smart content.

To know what and when to post, here's the secret: It's all about your unique target audience. At its core, social media content should be about offering free value that meets or resonates with the specific felt needs of your target audience. Social media allows you to position yourself as the go-to source for information and encouragement that adds value to the lives of your church members as well as the unchurched. If the content you post is not tailor-crafted for the specific audience you're targeting, you're missing the mark.

As the leader of a digital marketing agency, I usually see three main reasons for posting on social media. My guess is that every initiative you do at your church falls into one of these three buckets:

» To grow social media numbers and increase engagement.

» To grow email lists (for later communication about donations, attendance, special events, etc.).

» To compel the audience to do something (attend, give, invite others, share a post, etc.).

• If your goal is to grow your social media platform(s) . . .

You should be posting content that is easily shareable and invites engagement. Here's the breakdown:

1. **Easily shareable simply means content your audience will naturally want to share.** Consider the motives of your target audience and the reasons these people share content. What content can you give your audience that they will immediately want to share? What image or quote will they repost because it somehow makes them look or feel savvier, sharper, compassionate, or well-connected?

   Content suggestions: Include images with quotes, powerful Scripture, funny memes. Include a hashtag or a link in your post so that when someone shares it, you can easily bring traffic back to your church's website or other digital pages.

2. **"Invites engagement" describes content that sparks interest and invites dialogue.** Across all platforms, offer incentives to engage. Help people feel connected and known, or reward them for their comments.

   Content ideas: Ask questions that specifically invite a response, or incentivize responses and shares by offering a giveaway to those who respond. For example, you might post on Instagram, "Tell us your favorite verse! The first ten folks to comment will be entered to win Pastor John's new book!"

- If your goal is to grow your email list . . . . . .

Email marketing/communication can be very effective. Getting into someone's inbox gives you "permission" to talk to them, which has proven to generate more successful engagement and conversion (your audience is moved to action: buying, donating, attending, etc.) than just advertising or posting on a website.

The best part? You can easily use social media to grow your email list. If this is your goal, use your social media platforms to drive traffic to a landing page that features a piece of "gated content"—awesome content (a video series or eBook, for example) that your audience can download for free when they type in their email address. Be sure this "gated content" resource offers explicit value to your target audience. They get helpful information and insight, and you get their email address for future communication.

Content ideas: Keep your social media copy short and pithy, stating the benefits of the free resource. Be sure to include the website landing page link. Include in your posts images of the resource, as well as direct quotes or sneak peeks of the resource's content.

- If your goal is to motivate your audience to do something (attend, give, etc.) . . .

View social media as an awesome way to drive traffic to a website with all the information the audience will need to follow through on your "ask." Use Twitter, Facebook,

Instagram, and other platforms to engage audiences with compelling copy and a link. Remember that social media's job is not to do the convincing; rather, its job is to push traffic to the Web page that gives people the motivation and information they need to act.

The secret here is to use social media to spark interest and to occasionally remind your audience of the "ask." The majority of the work should happen on a strong, engaging Web page.

Content ideas: Leverage social media to tell your audience about freebies or bonuses associated with your "ask." Create urgency around these items (such as, "Sign up for the luncheon by tomorrow and get a free eBook with your registration!"). People are even more likely to engage when there's a tangible added value and a deadline.

∩ ∩ ∩ ∩

WHAT MAKES CONTENT "STICKY"?

Matt Brown, social media evangelist and strategist

We've all seen it—the cute cat video with a gazillion views, the silly meme that generates thousands of comments and "likes," etc. But why can't we seem to get our church posts to garner more than a few likes when, let's be honest, we are posting about the most important subject on earth?

Is superengagement on social media left only to those who play on Facebook all day long and know how to work the system? Or do we need to have unfathomable, superbudgets to reach millions of fans, leaving "viral" attainable only to a select few who are willing to break their bank?

As someone who works with ministries to build their social media platforms, I can offer you simple steps to share better, stickier content that more people will respond to—without spending money. (I do recommend setting a budget for social media because you can reach a lot of people with very little money, but that's a discussion for another time.)

However, before I get to the practical stuff, let me share a few insights about the inner workings of the various social media platforms.

Facebook: You should know that Facebook has a computer code called an algorithm that tracks how well your post does on your page, and then based on that performance and a lot of other factors, Facebook shows your post to more and more people if it gets positive responses. Typically a single post on a church's Facebook page will only reach 5 to 10 percent of the church's Facebook fans. However, over the course of a week, your "impressions" will likely reach somewhere close to your total page fans.

Twitter and Instagram: All of your followers do not see your posts on Twitter and Instagram, partly because they don't necessarily log in every day. So they miss your post among all the others. Other social media platforms either have incorporated, or will incorporate, similar algorithms to Facebook's, so it's important to know how to maximize your church's effectiveness against this reality.

Essentially, some content is "stickier" than others, and generates more response (likes, retweets, comments, shares, etc.). With a little effort, your church can learn how to create the best possible content to reach the most possible people (for example, triple the amount of people who typically see it).

- Seven Simple Steps to Create Sticky Content

   1. **Ask yourself, "Would I share this post?"** Chances are that if you wouldn't share your post, other people won't either. Make every post you do a great one. Consider adding an inspirational statement that will cause people to click "like," "retweet," "share," or "favorite." Always ask yourself: Would I share this post if I saw someone else post it?

   2. **Notice the posts people respond to and do more posts like that.** What posts did you recently do that generated a lot of "likes"? Based on the comments and response, what elements caused the post to do well? Include similar measures in your next post to copy some of the success of the previous ones.

   3. **Do less promotional posts—ask less of your followers.** Try to keep your church's social media pages from becoming newsletters or event listings. A good rule of thumb: Post event updates and news only once out of every three or four posts.

   4. **Share more inspiring content and offer your followers more value.** Most people, most of the time, want to read content on social media that inspires and encourages them. You can still bring the truth of God's Word, but do it in ways that uplift people and guide them throughout their week.

      Idea: Ask your pastor for the sermon notes from the last week and pull the top quotes and verses to use for posts. Throughout the week, these posts will remind people what and how God is speaking to your church.

   5. **Minimize the elements in your posts so they're easy**

to scan, agree with, and "like." Don't add too many hashtags (#) or website links. Use these tools sparingly. If you add a quote attribution, put it on the next line down and give it a dash (example: —Dr. Martin Luther King, Jr.). You don't even need quotation marks. The less people have to process, the easier it is to scan and agree with the post, and the better response it will get.

6. **For ten times better reach, upload your video directly to Facebook.** I recently posted a video on YouTube that received a few hundred views, and the same video to Facebook, which received thousands of views. A video on Facebook is a powerful tool.

   However, don't upload a YouTube link (Facebook and YouTube are competitors, so Facebook will automatically limit links from YouTube, Twitter, and other competitor sources). Instead, upload your video directly to Facebook. Give it a quick summary statement that people can quickly scan and agree with, and one that causes them to want to click "like" and share! Remember that most users' attention spans are about six minutes. If a video is long, it may take a while to upload—and then you've lost viewers. I'd even suggest picking a two- to three-minute clip from the weekly message to upload directly to Facebook, with a link to the full message on your church website.

7. **Post directly to each social media site.** As tempting as it is, don't connect your Facebook to your Twitter, or vice versa. If possible, it's better to post directly to each platform; your content will perform significantly better for overall reach. Sometimes I use platforms like Buffer and Hootsuite to schedule my Twitter posts, but as a

rule of thumb I try to schedule Facebook posts directly through Facebook. Each social media platform wants to keep you engaged directly on its site, so each rewards you for posting directly by causing your posts to be seen by more people.

With a little more effort, you can reach thousands more people with your church's message through social media each week. The results are worth the extra effort and the several extra minutes it takes to post individually. In fact, social media could be one of the most important time investments your team makes each week. Create great impressions for those following your church online, consistently encouraging and inspiring your audience. Through social media, show them the kind of quality experience they can expect if and when they drop by your church for a visit or begin to attend your weekly services.

Chapter 3
Story: Your Church's Story & God's Story

ALL OF THE BUZZ INDICATED THIS MOVIE WOULD BE A blockbuster for kids—the new trendsetter. So why was my four-year-old son bored stiff watching it? It was full of the latest and greatest high-dollar computer animation. It had an all-star cast. Hey, it was even built on a multimillion dollar franchise. Still, to my kid, none of these things mattered. He wanted it to be over. Done.

Fast-forward a few days. We're sitting at home, and the same four-year-old child is tired from playtime and wants to watch a movie. As I load in the seventy-six-year-old feature film, I fully expect a repeat of bored-kid syndrome. This antiquated movie wasn't produced with any modern technology or voice actors of renown. But this boy was captivated. He hung on every word. He didn't miss a scene.

That is the power of story.

Story goes to the core of who we are as humans. It unites us with ages past and casts vision to the future. Stories teach valuable lessons and communicate timeless truths. Think about it. The Great Commission is Christ calling us to go throughout the world as storytellers telling the greatest story ever told.

Social media is a communications tool—another tool in our arsenal as storytellers. Your church has a powerful opportunity to enter workplaces, subway cars, and homes with stories held in the palms of people's hands as they watch, listen, and read the stories you're telling on social media.

In this chapter, we're looking at a few questions you may have when it comes to storytelling in social media:

- Can social media be more than selfies and cat videos? (Carrie Kintz)

- How can I use social media to tell a bigger story? (Sam Hoover)

- What do I need to know to curate the right stories? (Mark Forrester)

—Mark Forrester

CAN SOCIAL MEDIA BE MORE THAN SELFIES AND CAT VIDEOS?

Carrie Kintz, social media strategist

I still remember when pastor and author Tim Keller joined Twitter a couple of years ago. In one of his early tweets, he shared with his rapidly growing audience that he was on Twitter because his son told him he had to be. I loved his transparency. At the time, his attitude seemed to reflect the general feelings of pastors and churches toward social media. No matter how much Keller seemed to be on Twitter against his will, he quickly captured the honesty and authenticity central to social media.

Since Facebook burst on the scene in 2004, businesses, governments, and churches have tried to figure out what it's good for. As we've already talked about in chapter 1, questions still swirl about how social media can actually help spread the gospel, grow churches, and create relationships. The hesitation is understandable. As social media continues to weave itself into the cracks and crevices of our lives, we seem to be more entertained by the newest cat gif on BuzzFeed or enduring another trending story about an outrageous selfie that Kim Kardashian posted on Instagram.

However, how others use social media doesn't change the fact that our churches have a place on social media. Beyond that, as Christians we have something and Someone far better to share about than the newest Carpool Karaoke video. (Although, admittedly, I do love Carpool Karaoke.) If you or your church is wondering if social media can help you tell a more meaningful story than videos of Fluffy's latest feat or a multitude of selfies, here are a few things to consider as you think about making it a part of your church communication strategy.

• Social Media Is about Stories

As churches, we have mission statements. We cast vision for where our congregations are going. Social media doesn't overshadow those things, but rather fits into them. It offers one more way you can play your part in the kingdom of God and invite others to come alongside you.

We have no idea how far some of the things we share online reach and how Jesus uses each one—both on this earth and eternally. When I worked at Focus on the Family, we received messages and posts thanking us for a verse we posted or a broadcast we shared on social media. People often expressed how that content was just what they needed in a hard moment, or that we had challenged them to look at issues differently. Their encouragement was a great reminder that no matter what color a silly dress was or which celebrity had just been arrested, we were a place where people could get help. We were actually ministering to people rather than adding to the Internet noise.

As the body of Jesus, we can't forget that we have not only the opportunity, but also the responsibility, to offer hope in a world so desperate for it. We can choose to use this tool for change and to proclaim the life-changing story of the gospel.

• Social Media Is about Connecting to Each Other's Stories

Online friendships and connections can become real-life relationships. I can't tell you how many people—Christian and not—I've met through Twitter. I have the opportunity to learn from some of the greatest communicators in the global church, as well as strengthen local ties. When forest fires ravaged Colorado Springs, Colorado, where I live, I connected with my community in a deeper way—all through online relationships.

The church has the chance to add to these kinds of conversations, not by broadcasting when services are happening, but by engaging people who are asking genuine questions about God or the Bible. And when that door opens, we can begin to turn that online connection into a real-life and eternal connection.

• Social Media Is Personal

The channels we're on give us another way to fulfill Jesus' Great Commission in Matthew 28. When you first enter the world of social media, remember that living and breathing people are behind the Twitter handles, Instagram photos, and Facebook posts. They hurt just like you do when someone makes a negative comment.

So instead of approaching a channel with the intent to broadcast or talk about your church, listen to people by reading their feeds first. As you see what people are sharing on a specific channel, you'll learn how to join conversations. Soon, you'll find your church engaging in someone else's story, offering to pray for someone halfway around the world, or chatting with another pastor about what you've planned for Vacation Bible School. When social media becomes personal for you and your church, it will revolutionize how you use the various channels.

——— A Case Study ———

Social Media in Action

How a City in Crisis Used Social Media to Tell Their Story

You may not remember the date, but chances are you remember the news headlines and video footage of forest fires ravaging the city of Colorado Springs, Colorado. In June 2012, the Rocky Mountains to the west of the city caught on fire. More than three hundred homes burned, and more than thirty-two thousand residents were displaced.

When news of the fire broke out, our county sheriff and fire department officials immediately began to use social media to share information. They quickly established an official hashtag, #WaldoCanyonFire, used social media monitoring tools, responded to misinformation, and became the hub of any new information. The Red Cross, local churches, schools, and citizens used the hashtag to broadcast information about shelters and resources. Colorado Springs residents quickly established patterns of communication, urging tweeters to check time stamps to make sure the news they were sharing was the most accurate and up-to-date. That week, on Twitter alone, more than twenty-five thousand unique users typed #WaldoCanyonFire into more than one hundred thousand messages—resulting in 54.4 million impressions of the hashtag over a fifteen-day period and a powerful display of how social media can help tell an important story and be used for the greater good.

— *C. K.*

ᕦ ᕦ ᕦ ᕦ

HOW CAN I USE SOCIAL MEDIA TO TELL A BIGGER STORY?

Sam Hoover, director of social media, Compassion International

When it comes to social media, often we want to create something brand-new. The "cool" factor begs us to do something worthy. Your church bulletin or website might never go viral, so you may be tempted to set apart the content you create for social media from the other content you create for your bulletin or newsletter. Realize that this kind of thinking takes social media in a different direction from everything else you do, and, unfortunately, is a recipe for failure. Don't set up social media as a competitor to your various forms of communication. Instead, social media should complement all of the content your church shares.

To do that, your social media strategy should fit into everything your church communicates, which means it must fit into a bigger story. So where does this bigger story exist? Thankfully, it might be closer than you think.

The best way to bring social media into a bigger story is to use it to help tell the three bigger stories already happening around you: your church's bigger story, your community's bigger story, and God's bigger story. Identifying each one is the first step in understanding how social media can complement—and not compete with—everything you do.

• Connect to Your Church's Bigger Story

There's a good chance your church has boiled down its work into one simple mission statement. At Compassion International, where I direct social media, our organization's mission statement is, "Releasing children from poverty in Jesus' name." Everything we do as an organization—from program and marketing to human resources and customer service—fits into this concise statement. That includes social media.

We use social media to help "release children from poverty in Jesus' name" by sharing the inspiring stories of the children we serve; encouraging and educating the sponsors and donors who follow us; and advocating for children in poverty to the general public. Every picture and video, post, and reply is aimed at furthering our mission.

- Connect to Your Community's Bigger Story

If you look long and hard at the community you live in, there's a good chance you'll see groups of people gathered around certain ideas. Your community is crawling with bigger stories. Maybe your city is a growing advocate for adoption and orphan care. Maybe your town creates opportunities for homeless outreach. Maybe your neighborhood emphasizes going green, recycling, and taking responsibility for our planet. Knowing your city's DNA can help you use your social media efforts to tell your community's bigger story. Find one or two of those stories and engage your social media efforts to tell it.

- Connect to God's Bigger Story

This might be the most obvious story of all three. It can look a bit like a Jesus juke (when someone takes what is clearly a joke-filled conversation and completely reverses direction into something serious and holy), but it's not. If your church incorporates Christian doctrine into everything you do, why shouldn't you include social media? If we meet, pray, and serve because the

Bible tells us to, maybe Scripture offers direction on how our social media can be guided as well.

Acts 1:8 says, "You will be my witnesses in Jerusalem, and in all Judea and Samaria, and to the ends of the earth." Unless you think that "ends of the earth" part is someone else's job (and it isn't), how will you do that? Maybe social media can help us be Christ's witnesses.

Matthew 5:14 says, "You are the light of the world. A town built on a hill cannot be hidden." Unless you think that part about the "world" is figurative (and it isn't), how will you and your church continue to cast light on the shadowy parts? Maybe social media can help us be light in darkness.

It might seem a bit trite, but the more you can connect your social media strategy to the words God has given us through Scripture, the better. Simply put, obeying God's bigger story can help you leverage your social media to tell a bigger story.

Integrating your plan for social media into a bigger story is the best way to set up your work for success. And the good news is that bigger stories are happening all around you. You simply need to find them and let social media help you tell them.

WHAT DO I NEED TO KNOW TO CURATE THE RIGHT STORIES?

Mark Forrester, senior director of public relations and communications, General Council of the Assemblies of God

Nestled in the woods of northwest Arkansas stands Crystal Bridges—an art museum funded by Walmart heiress, Alice Walton. The beautiful, extravagant museum introduces residents of rural Bentonville to unique treasures of American art that otherwise would have been largely out of reach to them.

But the museum didn't go up without controversy. As the curation process began, news media began buzzing. "What is Alice Walton thinking?" asked Artsjournal.com in an article published by that name. Soon, criticism piled on from *The Guardian*, *Bloomberg Review*, *The New Yorker*, and others. The main question: Why should public treasures from artists like Norman Rockwell, Andy Warhol, and Georgia O'Keeffe be placed in rural Arkansas?

It was a question of audience: Would a rural Arkansas population be able to appreciate the fine works of art the museum continued to curate? In the years since the museum opened, that question has been answered by the museum's amazing success. The curator knew the audience and met the need.

So what do we mean by "curation" in social media, and how do you use curated content to help you tell stories?

Similar to curating art, curation in social media involves listening to your audience, gathering information from outside sources, and occasionally commissioning pieces to present a clear perspective of a topic.

Imagine visiting a fine arts museum that only displayed pieces by its curator. That curator would soon be out of a job. The pressure on the curator is not to produce the right content, but to procure the right content. Your primary goal is to know your audience and provide them with the content that meets their needs and fits with your organization's mission.

Effective content curation also alleviates pressure from your daily posting schedule because you begin to build up a repository of compelling content. As a content curator for your church or organization, learning to curate the right content for your audience will add spice and vitality to your social media presence. You'll also find that it will add to more people sharing your content.

- Social Listening

When we practice social listening, we research to see what people are saying about a particular brand or topic. For example, when you set up a Google alert for a particular keyword (Google notifies you of new results that match your search term), you're "listening" for a mention of that word. Effective content curation begins with effective social listening. But this kind of listening can be overwhelming! (Refer to the Appendix Resource at the back of this book for recommendations on social listening tools.) Here, let's look at ways to make your listening more effective:

1. **Don't be overly broad.** When using a listening tool, remember that the more targeted your search is, the more relevant items you'll find. Familiarize yourself with the search tool you're using. Set the most appropriate keywords for what you're searching for—and if your search tool allows, set exclusions to help you streamline your specific search and cut through the white noise of irrelevant results.

2. **Separate the items you find according to task.** If you find something for reposting, either do it immediately or mark it for later. If you're planning to follow up for more information, flag the post for follow-up. With so much information coming at you, effective organization will be your best friend.

3. **Keep your searches current.** Listening isn't a one-and-done task. Regularly take inventory of your searches to see which ones need to be added, modified, or eliminated.

- Gather Leads from Outside Sources

Not every story you share will start with you—or even be about you! In fact, some of the most interesting and relatable stories you'll share may be happening outside your walls in your community. Here are a few ideas for searching out usable content from outside sources:

1. **Create lists.** This is one of the easiest and fastest ways to organize people or organizations into topical accounts. Twitter started early with the capability to create lists, and many other social networking sites soon followed. As a church, you may want to have a specific list set up for local schools, local businesses, and other influential voices in your community. Interacting with the people and organizations on these lists not only builds bridges to your community, it also provides you with a healthy stream of local content to repost or use as an idea for a new post. Setting up lists for group leaders, staff, or volunteers at your church can also alert you to amazing stories you might not have seen otherwise.

2. **Identify national voices of interest to your congregation.** You'll find that an inspiring quote related to your weekend service, or a story of life change from another church, can translate powerfully to your congregation.

3. **Monitor reliable Christian news sources.** Look for stories or breaking news that may be of interest to members of your church. Always remember to check the veracity of an article before posting it. With the abundance of satire sites and shoddy reporting, it's easy to share a credible-looking article that's far from legitimate.

- User-Generated Content

The double-edged sword of social media communications is that people want to talk about your church, organization, or brand! As we all eventually discover, that can be a very good thing or a very bad thing.

Not only can campaigns that encourage user-generated content provide great content for you to post or repost, they also give people an opportunity to spread positive talk about your church. Here are some basic ways your church can proactively encourage user-generated content:

>   Set up photo opportunities. Whether inside or outside your church, find visible locations to provide creative sets that will attract attendees to take photos.

>   Make it a contest. Ask people to submit photos, videos, or other pieces of storytelling content for a contest that matches a theme or objective your church is championing. Healthy competition can provide you with content fodder for the duration of the campaign.

>   Provide physical items that beg to be shared! Coca-Cola did this with excellence in its "Share a Coke" campaign that included customizable names and generic roles (Sister, Friend, Dad, etc.) imprinted on Coca-Cola products. Seeing the name of a friend automatically prompted sharing. *The Wall Street Journal* reported that this campaign was a major factor in the company's reversal of years of decline in domestic revenue.[1]

Whether creating it or gathering it, content will remain key in social media—just like any other communications venue. Make sure your curated content follows the same or better standards than the content you produce on your own.

Chapter 4
Connecting with Your Church

Imagine a place where:

no one felt alone;

everyone felt welcomed, wanted, and accepted;

people were prioritized over programs;

and every voice was heard.

Now imagine that you've been searching for a church community like this. A place that embraces the uniqueness of the person God has created you to be, a place that daily enriches your life, frequently encourages you, and makes you feel known. From the moment you enter this place to the moment you leave it, you know this is the community your soul desperately craves.

This is the church community that Jesus invites us into—an ecclesia. Today's church has the potential to be more connected to their ecclesia than ever before, as the local church brings the experience of the weekend into the daily lives of the church body. No longer is community fragmented or contingent on a single day of the week; connection can now be a seamless, enriching experience throughout the week—thanks to social media.

For many churches, connecting with their community through social platforms has been a difficult concept to grasp. We've confused social networks for mass communication platforms and as a result have developed mass communication strategies void of any personal touch. We've clung to the masses while leaving the individual behind.

But this is not how social media is supposed to work, and leaving out the individual person was never the desire or heart of Jesus. He often left the masses to go after the individual. Throughout Scripture, we see Jesus connecting with people on a personal level and walking with them through life transformation. As if that weren't enough, Jesus empowered and equipped the church with His Holy Spirit so that we could worship Him together as a community in the Spirit and in truth. This is the ecclesia the church is called to be—a community that leverages technology to empower, encourage, and equip each other as we live life together.

Jesus cared about people first, and as the church, we should be the best at practicing true community through our social networks. It's time to connect your local church body to the heart and spirit of your church—one person at a time.

In this chapter, we're answering specific questions to help you create, enhance, and maintain tight community within your church:

- Are multiple social media accounts better than a single account from my church? (Allyson Siwajian)

- How do I use social media as a tool to foster community? (José Huergo)

- How do I tap into volunteer potential to manage social media? (Haley Veturis)

ARE MULTIPLE SOCIAL MEDIA ACCOUNTS BETTER THAN A SINGLE ACCOUNT FROM MY CHURCH?

Allyson Siwajian, digital engagement and communications liaison,The Foursquare Church

Every strong community needs a place to come together to thrive. In the digital era, social media provides that space to cultivate community online. But as you take the plunge to create that digital space for your church, think about how it is best to start. Sure, you want your church to have a social media account. But how many accounts?

Let me pause to share the differences between a social media account and a social media platform. A social media platform is a medium, a venue, a hosting ground. Think Facebook, Twitter, Instagram, YouTube. A social media account is a profile. It's your personal page, your zone on any platform, your house on the block. Think church name, youth group name, your own name.

Your church can establish a presence on many platforms. But how many accounts per platform should you have? Would you benefit from having multiple accounts, or just one central hub?

Many church leadership teams are quick to open multiple social media accounts. That way, each team leader gets to control his or her own content, posting whatever, whenever. But while multiple accounts on one platform can gift ownership, ask yourself why your church is on social media in the first place.

It's about community.

Let me give you a little illustration. When I watch a movie, I don't want to experience just one element of the film. To create a complete movie-watching experience, I need to experience everything—visual effects, dialogue, musical score, cinematography, etc.—in sync. To produce a movie, the whole film crew has to bring together all of their independent roles. When thinking about your church's social media efforts, think beyond your individual parts. Consider the audience and what's best for their experience. Below, I share a few benefits for having a single account (versus multiple accounts) on a social media platform:

» A single account allows you to deliver a more complete image of who you are as a church. Your church is more than Sunday sermons and motivational Scriptures. Your profile can feature all of who you are: worship and world missions, neighborhood picnics and city outreach, discipleship and Communion, men and women, kids and youth. Variety keeps members engaged and excited, and it shows potential guests you're no one-trick pony.

» A single account doesn't ask the average church attendee to follow seventeen different accounts to receive news for one church. If you wouldn't print seventeen different bulletins, don't start seventeen different accounts. Instead, allocate space to every ministry in your church and develop a process that each ministry can use to submit content to an account facilitator. As you begin, try themed days for your profile, such as "Youth Group Thursdays" or "Missional Community Mondays." Then, your account is organized (just like a good bulletin or announcement video), making it easy to access all updates in one place.

» A single account encourages attendees to think beyond their immediate spheres. As the church, we celebrate diversity even as we stay united. If you want to connect attendees to the whole church mission (versus an individual ministry or part of the church), give people a chance to see and engage with content that otherwise may have never crossed their radar. For example, posting a photo showing lives changed at summer camp could compel someone to sponsor a student next season.

Of course, there are always exceptions to any rule. Could it be possible to need more than one account? Perhaps. To know if you need multiple accounts per platform, consider the answers to these questions:

» Are our church members über tech savvy? Are they eager to get all the news, all the time, and, yes, they know about "notifications"?
» Do I lead a church whose ministries regularly exceed one thousand people?
» Does our church have more than one campus?
» Do the ministries at our church have their own websites, apart from the church website?
» As the leader of the church, do I want a personal presence online, separate from our church account?

If you answered yes to any of those questions, now you can talk about setting up more than one account on any of the platforms you choose.

Ultimately, you know your church best. Look to foster community in a healthy, life-giving way for both attendees and staff. Then use social media for its best possible design: sharing God's story as it plays out through your church.

○ ○ ○ ○

HOW DO I USE SOCIAL MEDIA AS A TOOL TO FOSTER COMMUNITY?

José Huergo, brand manager, Hillsong Worship

I like to think of social media as a tool to reach and influence the world. Some use it to build and encourage, others to bring people down. As Christians, we have a responsibility to set an example by showing kindness and adding value to the lives of those who follow us on social media, which in most cases are our very own congregations.

Let's explore a few ways we can use this tool to foster community, and look at some practical examples of how we can leverage it to create genuine connections with our audiences.

• Keep people posted without overposting (connecting with your church).

Make your audience feel included by keeping them informed. Let them know about special events coming up at your church and ways they can be involved. You can also use social media to build expectation leading up to your weekend services. Post often enough to build your audience, but don't post just for the sake of posting (a.k.a. spam). Get to know your audience and align your content with who they are and what they relate and respond to. Post at times when most are online.

Here are some practical ways to do this: Develop a schedule for posting. You'll begin to find a rhythm and identify the specific content you'll need. Think about the week or month ahead and plan your messaging content. Identify prime times for posting. For example:

>> Friday: Use posts to create excitement around your weekend services, the speaker, or the current sermon series.

>> Saturday/Sunday: Invite people to church, giving them a reason to come expectant. Remind them of weekend service times and locations.

>> Monday: Share highlights and Scripture from the weekend. Celebrate what God is doing in and through your church.

>> Tuesday through Thursday: Post Scriptures, quotes, or information about midweek activities like small groups and youth ministry.

Remember there's no set formula for posting on social media. So look for what works for you and your church, and then focus on improving the "how you do it" piece rather than trying to figure out what to do each time.

• Be social on social media (your church connecting with you).

While you want to keep your audience informed, social media is not just a broadcasting tool or an extension of the church bulletin board. Believe it or not, social media can be used as a tool to shepherd and teach people. You can encourage and inspire your congregation by speaking to their Monday life— not only their Sunday life. This kind of consistent connection requires us to be social on social media. To engage in genuine, encouraging exchanges, we first have to initiate and participate in more meaningful back-and-forth conversations. Social media is a two-way street. Don't let anyone try to tell you different.

Here are some practical ways to offer encouragement through social media:

» Regularly read through your church's official hashtags, liking and commenting on posts from attendees. One "like," comment, retweet, or share goes a long way when it comes from a church leader or church account.

» Honor and acknowledge people on social media, whether it's your senior pastor who just preached brilliantly, or highlighting and thanking volunteers for their involvement in worship services and ministries.

• Be a conversation catalyst (your church connecting with each other).

Social media can spark real-life conversations. On various platforms, you can share thought leadership and compelling content that your audience may want to share to encourage their own followers, or use as an invitation to your church events. To inspire advocacy, aim to communicate as clearly as possible at a consistently high standard. One caution: Think about the direct and indirect messages your posts send. While content can inspire, it can also invite criticism that could be avoided by paying attention to your words and tone. I often refer to Ephesians 4:29 when I'm writing captions or commenting on social media: "Let everything you say be good and helpful, so that your words will be an encouragement to those who hear them" (NLT). If a post doesn't align with Paul's challenge to the church of Ephesus, it doesn't go online. Post above reproach.

Here are some practical ways to use social media to ignite conversation:

» Share beautiful artwork in your posts that others would want to share on their social media feeds.

» Create hashtags to stimulate conversation around topics your church is studying (for example, #Godlymarriage) or campaigns your church is running. Encourage audiences to engage and share.

A Case Study

Social Media in Action

Rethinking Social Content to Build Church Engagement

In 2014, Hillsong Church was due for a social media restructure thanks to the unprecedented growth we had experienced. We had hundreds of social media accounts, and keeping up with all of them was proving to be challenging.

We decided to structure our accounts in line with the organizational structure of our church, which resulted in deleting numerous accounts and making others unofficial. Our current structure is Global Accounts, Official Local Accounts, and Unofficial Community Accounts, each with their respective parameters.

To implement our new strategy, we visually rebranded all of our accounts and established new naming conventions for all three levels to ensure we reach the intended target audience while streamlining our communication.

To help with the changes, we created images for our different church locations. As people walked through the doors of our church, they saw a large "Welcome Home" sign on the screens promoting the correct accounts to follow. We also communicated how the changes would make our content relevant to them. Since going through this renovation, we have experienced a higher level of church engagement. We are now posting the right content to the right people at the right times.

The temptation with social media can be to try to reach as many people as possible, rather than communicating strategically and purposefully. Remember that large numbers of followers don't necessarily guarantee deep and authentic relationships.

— *J. H.*

∩ ∩ ∩ ∩

HOW DO I TAP INTO VOLUNTEER POTENTIAL TO MANAGE SOCIAL MEDIA?

Haley Veturis, social media manager, Saddleback Church

For many churches with little or no budget to hire a social media manager, volunteers (usually young people) can be that "staff member" who can ignite and continue to develop your social media presence. But before you can tap into latent volunteer potential in your church, you first need to know these potential volunteers and understand how God has gifted each person who may serve.

At Saddleback Church, our church culture sets the expectation that every member serves in a ministry. Pastor Rick Warren consistently reinforces serving (one of our core beliefs and one of five foundational purposes of our church), noting the potential power of mobilizing God's people: "If we can ever awaken and unleash the massive talent, resources, creativity, and energy lying dormant in the typical local church, Christianity will explode with growth at an unprecedented rate."

- Identifying and Recruiting Potential Volunteers

Each of us has unique abilities, personality, experience, passion, and spiritual gifts to contribute. Some people may have a heart for social media, but their ability, personality, and experiences may not be a good fit. Get to know the people at your church to discover how you can help them unleash their potential.

If you want to learn about more people in a short time, a questionnaire is a great tool for discovering likely candidates. Some helpful yet basic introductory questions for potential social media volunteers include:

> » Which social networks are you on?
> » Which social networks do you enjoy most?
> » Which social networks do you enjoy least?
> » What are you passionate about?
> » How do you see yourself serving the church through this ministry?

Searching your social feed is another good way to identify the social influencers in your church. Chances are you already have people actively engaged with your church through social media. Now it's just a matter of giving them the opportunity to do what they're already doing, in the context of ministry. Remember that this is not about recruiting more people for your ministry, but rather motivating more people to pursue and cultivate a servant heart. Show volunteers and potential volunteers the big picture of what they're doing for the church. Every volunteer is important; every role has a higher purpose. When people see what they're contributing to, they're more likely to invest their time and effort to help.

- Equipping and Structuring Your Social Media Volunteer Team

Across the board, tapping into volunteer potential is done best when volunteers are both equipped and empowered to do the job. From church-facilitated workshops to simple one-on-one coaching, many methods are available to equip volunteers to serve.

Maximizing your volunteer social media efforts requires you to communicate clear pathways of serving and growing within the ministry. At Saddleback, we've established three ways to serve through our social media team.

1. **Advocate.** Every member serves as an advocate for the church. Advocates share their church experiences through their own social channels by posting photos to Instagram, populating church or series-specific hashtags, live-tweeting content from the weekend message, or by sharing posts from our church's Facebook Fan Page. Anyone who is active on social media can serve as an advocate.

2. **Social media expert.** This is a great fit for volunteers with more knowledge, experience, and a notable social media presence. This volunteer position requires greater commitment than an advocate and is tasked with more responsibilities. Social media experts serve the church by aiding with community management of the social channels. They are empowered to respond to posts—following the voice, style, and strategy of our church. Volunteers on this level should have a clear understanding of how to communicate in the voice of the church and have a heart for serving. If your church values high engagement and two-way communication, this position is crucial.

3. **Social media champs.** Volunteers who exhibit all of the qualities mentioned above and are passionate about the church serve as social media champs. Champs run the social media channels for our church and are responsible for posting as Saddleback Church, following the church's social strategy and fostering community online throughout the week. This position requires the highest level of commitment and responsibility. We intentionally appoint no more than two social media champs at each campus to ensure consistency and quality across the board. These volunteers are top-notch.

Additionally, here's a look at how other churches throughout the country mobilize volunteers for social media efforts.

- » At The Rock Church in San Diego, social media volunteers curate content from their local campuses, live-tweet during campus events, as well as monitor and reply to comments and questions, just as a community manager would.
- » At National Community Church in Washington, DC, volunteers manage campus Facebook fan pages, write and send weekly campus newsletters, and curate content on the latest news for social justice initiatives the church is heavily involved in and advocates.
- » Sandals Church in Riverside, California, and Community Bible Church in San Antonio, Texas, both equip and empower volunteers to schedule content for social posts, respond to mentions and comments, and aid in content curating of weekend messages/podcasts.

Ultimately, our churches should care more about people than about getting tasks done. Always put the people in your church before projects and rely on God to provide the right people for your social media team. Remember, people are not distractions from ministry; they are your ministry!

Chapter 5
Reaching Your Community

AARON BURKE KNEW THAT THE SOUTH TAMPA, FLORIDA, area was his missions field. During the course of his research on the area, he discovered that a whopping 87 percent of the population there had absolutely no church affiliation. He was determined to change that.

Others had been equally determined in the past, but had little to no success in the South Tampa community. In fact, some had called the area a "graveyard" of church plants. But Burke's small team of seventeen had a different plan—a strategy passionately birthed by prayer and practically implemented by Facebook.

As the optimistic troop pushed ahead with a well-executed social media plan, they started seeing people show up, curious about what was happening in their own backyard. Then the testimonies started coming. Lives were being changed as a result of Radiant Church's social media strategy! Soon, that small group of seventeen grew to nearly one thousand people, making a significant impact in South Tampa.[1]

Social media is equal parts art and science—and zero parts magic. Don't let anyone tell you different. As with any form of communication, we must give painstaking attention to make sure our choice of words and images are appropriately reaching our community and resonating in our specific context. Beyond that are concrete, measurable strategies your church can implement to reach your community more effectively through social media.

In this chapter, we'll address a few questions you may have about reaching your community through social media:

- How do I get to the people I'm trying to reach with social media? (Nate Smoyer)

- What can we do to amplify the special events at our church? (Clark Campbell)

- How do we leverage social media to create a social movement in our community? (Austin Graff)

—Mark Forrester

HOW DO I GET TO THE PEOPLE I'M TRYING TO REACH WITH SOCIAL MEDIA?

Nate Smoyer, digital marketing specialist

Whether we're trying to activate our church members or reach out to members of our community, we all face limitations or barriers—personnel, financial, even know-how—to reaching our intended audience.

That's the power of social media. It offers anyone—individual or church—the ability to leverage existing resources to reach both the church and the community. In this chapter, we're talking about reaching your community. But before we get into the "how," I want to focus on the "why"—why your church should leverage social media to reach your surrounding community. Here are a few top reasons:

> » To engage the segment of your community that doesn't attend church
> » To share stories of revival through Jesus
> » To provide useful information, such as helpful services for the poor
> » To distribute biblical teaching and application from the weekend sermon
> » To be a light, a beacon that shines the truth of Jesus Christ

You may have ten more "whys" to add to this list, but remember that whatever the reasons, they should stem from your church's stated purpose and mission. Social media can help drive initiatives, but those initiatives should align with your church's overall goals. Below, I share a seven-step guide to leverage social media to reach your ideal audience.

- Know your "whys" and make sure everyone else knows them as well.

These will guide you how to leverage social media. Work with your church staff, board, and pastor to ensure what you're doing is in line with why you're doing it.

- Determine what reaching your desired audience would look like in simple but decisive terms.

Be as specific as possible. Simply gaining "likes" from your church on Facebook doesn't matter much. Perhaps a better indicator of success would be the number of "likes" from your city. Use SMART goals as a framework for defining success (see page 38).

- Identify potential core channels and then focus! #FocusWins

This step is just what it sounds like. Whether you have one volunteer who can give an hour or two a week or a full-time staff person to run your social media, you still have limited time and energy. Knowing which available channel is best suited to reach your intended audience and then focusing on that channel will help optimize your efforts. Channels can be social media platforms like Facebook or Twitter, worship announcements, events, newsletters, etc.

- Strategize your approach.

Don't let strategy scare you. It doesn't have to be complex. I like to keep my social media strategy plans to one page. Your strategy for reaching your intended audience will include information from steps 1–3. I use the outline method I learned as a third grader to keep my plans as simple as possible.

- Execute with precision (or as best you can).

An organized, well-timed, and precise execution of a plan can make all the difference. The execution step puts all your ideas and strategies to the test.

- Measure your efforts with brutal honesty.

Remember when we established our indicators of success in step 2? When you measure the impact of your campaign, look to see how well you achieved the initial goals and objectives you established at the onset.

- Learn and adjust.

In step 3, you identified what you thought would be your core channels for achieving your campaign goals and objectives. If you didn't achieve these goals, adjust your approach for the next push. Consider focusing on different channels, or increase your focus on the channels that performed best. This step should involve leaders in a candid, thirty-minute meeting to debrief and move forward.

Remember your whys and stay focused. Being on every social network isn't important. It's not your job to be everywhere and burn all your energy and resources on creating shared images, knowing the latest social craze app, and attempting to run complicated social engagement campaigns.

Effectively leveraging social channels to reach your surrounding community is about making sure your members know about the marriage conference price promotion and encouraging them to invite unchurched friends. It's about encouraging students to bring friends to the summer retreat. It's about providing local families all the information they need to attend an Easter service. You get the picture!

——— A Case Study ———

Social Media in Action

How One Ministry Used Social Media to Reach Its Global Community[2]

The challenge was simple for the young adult ministry Ekklesia: raise five thousand dollars to fund a freshwater project for the nonprofit organization Charity: Water in ninety days. Albeit simple, the campaign would not be easy to execute since most of the money would come from college students. Following the guide I outlined above, below is a play-by-play description of how we effectively reached our target audience:

1. We pursued a common cause and mission to give to those in need as an act of stewardship and worship, to the glory of God. We also leaned on Ekklesia's mission statement, which drives all of the church's ministry initiatives: "To create an authentic Christian community that effectively reaches out to unchurched people in love, acceptance, and forgiveness so that they may experience the joy of salvation and a purposeful life of discipleship."

2. Our goal was straightforward: raise five thousand dollars to build a freshwater well through Charity: Water.

3. We defined our initial core channels, in order of priority, as:

> »   Worship night announcements
> »   Facebook and Instagram

» Events on the Western Washington University campus

» Parent church announcements

We built momentum by leading with announcements of something big to come, leveraging Facebook events to invite students, who in turn were encouraged to invite their friends (both Christian and non-Christian), and sharing teaser photos on Instagram of Charity: Water merchandise we planned to sell on our launch night.

4. Our strategy was to raise a few hundred dollars a week through microevents that all focused on sharing with people the need for freshwater projects and communicating where their money would go. We drew people to these events using our primary and secondary core channels. We raised funds through the purchases of merchandise and other donated goods.

5. Because volunteers drove all of our event efforts, it was imperative that everyone be all-in with what we were trying to accomplish—and they were! Stellar volunteer efforts—showing up on time, actively sharing on social media about our microevents, and personally giving to the cause—were major contributing factors to the success of these events. Our first microevent raised $1,200 towards our campaign goal.

6. At the end of our campaign, measuring the results of our efforts was easy: Did we raise five thousand dollars? We raised $5,281! Measuring the effect of each microevent as we went along was an important piece to the overall campaign. We kept our strategy flexible, allowing us to call an audible as needed.

7. We learned that having a core team passionately dedicated to reaching our campaign goal was vital. And we learned how to better engage some of our students. One thing we hadn't anticipated was the increased sense of community. Years later, I still see people wearing the merchandise we created to fund the water well. We all bonded over that and our joint effort in being good stewards in the name of Christ.

— *N. S*

ค ค ค ค

WHAT CAN WE DO TO AMPLIFY THE SPECIAL EVENTS AT OUR CHURCH?

Clark Campbell, founder of SocialLion, Inc.

As you read through this chapter, you'll discover how community is one of the most fundamental and accepted ideas in our Christian faith. Unfortunately, when you couple the word *community* with *digital*, it often gets a bad rap. We have a hard time wrapping our minds around the significance of what digital community—often labeled fake or shallow—really looks like.

Traditionally, community has happened around some sort of physical presence at an event or gathering where people share experiences as they participate together and become a stronger community. While we're clearly aware of the substantial differences between physical interactions versus digital interactions, the potential for human emotion via digital communication is still very much a reality.

For example, walk with me for a moment. You've traveled with your church's youth group to the Grand Canyon, and you're all standing at the bottom near the Colorado River trying to make sense of the majestic beauty—the jagged rock formations, the towering cliffs, and the raging rapids running through all of it.

Hopefully, you just felt a touch of emotion as you pictured this experience. Now contrast that with a different experience. You're at home and see a picture or video of your youth group at the Grand Canyon saying, "Hey friends, check out this unbelievable thing we're experiencing right now! God is so huge, and this is so crazy! #WhoaGod" Chances are you'd still feel some emotion as you viewed the experience through a digital lens. At that moment, what's happening with your youth group community becomes a shared experience. No, you weren't necessarily standing with the group thousands of miles away, but you were . . . in a way, right?

Every week, you have countless opportunities for "Whoa, God!" moments in your church or ministry! So, how do we translate these emotions and shared experiences of ongoing ministry events to our digital community? Short answer—through pictures on the screen. At that point, we give our church community the opportunity to be part of the shared experience in real time rather than the next Sunday! Below, I offer a transferable process for amplifying events in your ministry:

» Identify stories that appeal to your broader digital community. Look for groups of people sharing in the experience—laughing, smiling, crying, dancing, celebrating, or collaborating.

» Identify the best social media platforms for amplifying these shared experiences. For your church, that might be Facebook and Instagram rather than Twitter. For other churches, it might be Snapchat rather than

Facebook. Don't choose a social media platform because you think it's cool. Look for where your community has set up residence and leverage those platforms. Do your homework before you amplify.

» Encourage the community at the event to amplify their perspective to their digital community. The more people that amplify the shared experience, the more likely the algorithms will increase your ministry reach.

» Identify the best time to amplify your shared experiences. Typically, it's best to share early afternoon, but algorithms can alter that timing. So measure the reach of your posts over time and, if necessary, experiment with posting at different times for the greatest reach.

» Engage people in your digital community—when they like, comment, share, retweet, repost, screen shot (Snapchat), or react (Facebook) to one or more of your posts. Reply to their comments, follow them, make a friend request, etc.

A Case Study
Social Media in Action

How One Ministry Used One Video to Multiply Its Reach and Amplify Its Message

A ministry recently asked our company, SocialLion, to amplify their event. They knew their content would be very powerful, and they wanted it to reach the broader community. Unfortunately, they didn't expect a large on-site attendance so from the beginning we were working against the odds. We decided to get creative and find the path of least resistance.

Here's what we did, step-by-step:

1. We chose to post on the ministry's larger Facebook page based on the number of existing fans. (Some ministries have multiple pages, so in this case I recommend using the page with the largest number of fans; you'll understand why in a second.)

2. We posted a video from the live event on the Facebook page. Then we clicked the Facebook Live icon (after publishing our video).

3. We created a compelling description of the video, answering the vital question, "What's in it for the viewer to click on this video and watch it?"

4. We posted to tag-appropriate ministries by using @_____.

5. We posted the Live status.

6. We asked the twenty to thirty attendees at the event to pull out their phones and share the Facebook Live video we had just posted.

7. We shared the post from other ministry channels.

Remember: only about thirty people were on-site for the actual event. The results were:

Views: That night, the video we posted on Facebook Live was viewed more than four hundred times. Do the math! Following the seven simple steps above, we amplified our message to approximately ten times the on-site audience size.

Reach: With this one video post, over a few days we reached two thousand-plus people—more than sixty-six times the size of the on-site audience. A few simple social media tricks amplified the message in a pretty significant way.

I chose this example intentionally. This was a small event from a very small ministry with a very small number of Facebook fans. These same results are attainable for you. All it took was leveraging two realities: (1) video is the most thumb-stoppable/compelling content; and (2) your fans have far greater potential to amplify your message than you do alone!

— *C. C.*

◠ ◠ ◠ ◠

HOW DO WE LEVERAGE SOCIAL MEDIA TO CREATE A SOCIAL MOVEMENT IN OUR COMMUNITY?

Austin Graff, social media and influence marketing, Honest Tea

If there's one thing I've learned about social media, it's this: Social media is all about human connection. Virtually every social media platform was initially created for human connections and relationships. Facebook was started to connect friends in college and grew to connect families and friends. Twitter began as a way to connect with influencers. Social media gives us the opportunity to show up, be seen, and connect with other people, a community. However, the question remains: How does a church connect with real people and foster community on social media?

While I led social media at International Justice Mission (IJM), the largest human rights organization trying to end slavery, human trafficking, and other forms of violence against the poor, our social media followers grew from zero to five hundred thousand—on no budget. We lacked the dollar signs, but we didn't lack connection. We deployed a strategy centered on connecting with our social media fans/followers by doing these things:

- We deployed the 80/20 rule.

Eighty percent of our content across all social platforms were "gives" to our social media followers, whether it an inspiring graphic, a free resource, or a creative video. These posts had no "ask," which allowed us to devote only 20 percent of our posts to asking our social fans to take action. Social media is like an actual relationship. If someone you met at a church event only communicated with you when they wanted something, you'd start to avoid that person. Social media is the same, which is why it's important to create the best practice of giving to your fan base. Develop your social media content strategy around the 80/20 rule!

- We reached out to new followers.

We tweeted at new followers. We asked them questions. We retweeted their posts. We celebrated them. The result? An army of loyalists who shared our content without being asked. Because of our loyal fans, we had one of the highest engagement rates for a nonprofit organization on Facebook.

- We treated social media as a customer-service arm and took it seriously.

We interacted with the vast majority of tweets and Facebook comments. Tip: Use the "favorite" button on Twitter if you don't want to retweet something. It's a great way to tell your social fans that you saw their tweet and appreciate it. Answer any question asked of you on social media. If someone asked you a question on the street, it would be rude to just walk by, right?

•   We activated influencers to share our content.

An influencer isn't just a celebrity or a professional athlete. I see influencers as one of three people:

> »   A celebrity. This can be anyone from your local news-caster to a national television announcer.
> »   A person with a social following of three thousand-plus.
> »   Anyone who frequently shares your content.

Reach out to influencers. Foster the relationship. Meet them face-to-face. Invite them to a private Facebook group where you give them the inside track to your ministry and ask them to share marquee content. Investing in influencers will help encourage others to join your community!

•   We used Twitter to connect with new audiences.

There's a time and place to create your own hashtag (for example, around events), but the goal of a hashtag is to reach new audiences. Research the top daily trends on Twitter. A great place to start is on the home page of your Twitter account in the lower left-hand corner. Use the hashtags you find there, if they're relevant. Also, Twitter gives you access to people you may otherwise not have access to. Research your local celebrities, newscasters, and businesses and reach out to them on Twitter, inviting them to events or asking them to share your content.

Of course, a good social media strategy will include beautiful, inspiring content and will leverage the newest social media technology or app. But at the end of the day, those things are lost without human connection and a community. My favorite author and TED Talks speaker, Brené Brown, says, "I define connection as the energy that exists between people when they feel seen, heard, and valued; when they can give and receive without judgment; and when they derive sustenance and strength from the relationship." Considering Brené is active on Twitter (@BreneBrown), I know she'd agree her quote applies to social media, too!

A Case Study

Social Media in Action

How One Ministry Leveraged Social Media to Ignite a Movement

"Our fight against human trafficking is one of the great human rights causes of our time." In 2012, President Barack Obama used these words in his speech to the Clinton Global Initiative (CGI). His speech was the first entirely dedicated to the issue of slavery by a major world leader since Abraham Lincoln!

What inspired President Obama to deliver such a speech? Part of the reason was the impact of the International Justice Mission's (IJM) first-ever digital letter writing campaign. Our goal was to ask seventy-two thousand Americans to sign a letter asking the President to take a stronger stance on helping to end modern-day slavery. As IJM's social media lead, my team and I knew it would take an entire community to reach our goal. That's why we deployed a social strategy with two major components:

Social activation: We worked hard to make sure social media was integrated throughout the entire campaign. We added social sharing buttons for people once they signed the letter with auto-messaging (shortened link and key hashtags). We literally saw hundreds of people use the sharing buttons every day.

Community management: Because our social strategy already used the 80/20 rule, our community was ready to act when asked. Every time someone tweeted about the campaign, we tweeted them to thank and challenge them to get five friends to sign the letter. We invited our top social media fans and influencers to share the campaign and resourced them with graphics, tracked links, and lots of love!

The most interesting part to all of this was that we spent zero dollars on marketing and promotion. If you work for a church that has no social budget, there is hope. There is a way. You can still start a movement!

— *A. G.*

ENDNOTES

Chapter 1 Why Social Media?

[1] http://www.nielsen.com/us/en/insights/reports/2015/the-total-audience-report-q1-2015.html

[2] Marshall McLuhan, *Understanding Media* (Berkeley, CA: Gingko Press, 2013).

[3] http://www.convinceandconvert.com/social-media-research/11-shocking-new-social-media-statistics-in-america/

[4] Shane Hipps, *Flickering Pixels* (Grand Rapids, MI: Zondervan, 2009).

[5] http://www.pewinternet.org/2015/10/08/social-networking-usage-2005–2015/

[6] http://www.lifeway.com/pastors/2015/09/01/research-finds-few-pastors-give-up-on-ministry/

[7] http://www.pewresearch.org/fact-tank/2013/10/16/12-trends-shaping-digital-news/

Chapter 3 Story: Your Church's Story & God's Story

[1] Mike Estrel, "'Share a Coke' Credited With a Pop in Sales," *The Wall Street Journal*, September 24, 2014.

Chapter 5 Reaching Your Community

[1] Ken Walker, "Church Planting Takes to Social Media," *PE News*, February 29, 2016.

[2] http://komonews.com/archive/not-just-a-drop-in-the-well-local-church-group-aims-to-raise-thousands-for-charitywater

RESOURCES APPENDIX

The contributors have recommended books, websites, blogs, platforms, and other helpful tools to ignite or bolster your church's social media presence.

Books

101 Social Media Tactics for Nonprofits: A Field Guide, Melanie Mathos and Chad Norman (Wiley), 2012.

The Art of Social Media: Power Tips for Power Users, Guy Kawasaki and Peg Fitzpatrick (Portfolio), 2014.

#AskGaryVee: One Entrepreneur's Take on Leadership, Social Media & Self-Awareness, Gary Vaynerchuk (HarperCollins), 2016.

Bird by Bird: Some Instructions on Writing and Life, Anne Lamott (Anchor), 1995.

Brief: Make a Bigger Impact by Saying Less, Joseph McCormack (Wiley), 2014.

The Checklist Manifesto: How to Get Things Right, Atul Gawande (Picador), 2011.

Contagious: Why Things Catch On, Jonah Berger (Simon & Schuster), 2013.

Groundswell: Winning in a World Transformed by Social Technologies, Charlene Li and Josh Bernoff (Harvard Business Review Press), 2011.

Hooked: How to Build Habit-Forming Products, Nir Eyal and Ryan Hoover (Portfolio), 2014.

Influence: The Psychology of Persuasion, Robert B. Cialdini (Harper Business), 2006.

Jab, Jab, Jab, Right Hook: How to Tell Your Story in a Noisy Social World, Gary Vaynerchuk (HarperBusiness), 2013.

Less Chaos. Less Noise: Effective Communications for an Effective Church, Kem Meyer, 2016.

Life Together: The Classic Exploration of Christian in Community, Dietrich Bonhoeffer (HarperOne), 1954.

Love Is the Killer App: How to Win Business and Influence Friends, Tim Sanders (Crown Business), 2003.

Made to Stick: Why Some Ideas Survive and Others Die, Chip Heath and Dan Heath (Random House), 2008.

Open Leadership: How Social Technology Can Transform the Way You Lead, Charlene Li (Jossey-Bass), 2010.

Platform: Get Noticed in a Noisy World, Michael Hyatt (Thomas Nelson), 2012.

Rewired: How Using Today's Technology Can Bring You Back to Deeper Relationships, Real Conversations and the Age-Old Methods of Sharing God's Love, Brandon Cox (Charisma House), 2014.

The Social Church: A Theology of Digital Communication, Justin Wise (Moody Publishers), 2014.

Social Media Explained: Untangling the World's Most Misunderstood Business Trend, Mark W. Schaefer, 2014.

Start.: Punch Fear in the Face, Escape Average, and Do Work That Matters, Jon Acuff (Ramsey Press), 2013.

Start With Why: How Great Leaders Inspire Everyone to Take Action, Simon Sinek (Portfolio), 2011.

Traction: How Any Startup Can Achieve Explosive Customer Growth, Gabriel Weinberg and Justin Mares (Portfolio), 2015.

Tribes: We Need You to Lead Us, Seth Godin (Portfolio), 2008.

Twitter for Good: Change the World One Tweet at a Time, Claire Díaz-Ortiz (Jossey-Bass), 2011.

Social Media Websites

Fast Company

Hubspot

Inbound.org

Mashable's Social Media section

Newsroom.fb.com

Nextdoor.com

Pew Research Center (Internet, Science and Tech section)

Skillshare

Thalamus

Upworthy

The Verge (Tech section)

Social Media Platforms

Beme

Facebook

Instagram

GodTube

LinkedIn

Periscope

Pinterest

Snapchat

Storify

Strava

Tumblr

Twitter

YouTube

Social Media Blogs

Buffer blog
Case Foundation
Chadwick Cannon
ChurchMag
The Content Strategist
Convince and Convert
DigitalMarketer.com
Dustin.tv
GrowthHackingIdea
Hootsuite Social Blog
Jon Acuff: Work Can Be Awesome
Jon Loomer
Mailchimp blog
The Moz Blog
Seth Godin
Social Media Examiner
Social Media Today

Other Helpful Tools

Scheduling/Reporting

Buffer
Facebook Scheduling
HootSuite
OnlyPult
ScheduGram
SproutSocial

Photo Gathering

Gratisography
Picjumbo
The Stocks
Unsplashk

Photo Editing

Fotor (photo editor and collage creation)
GIPHY (sharing GIFs in texts)
InstaSize (photo resizing)
Landscape (photo resizing)
Nik Collection (photo editing software)
Phonto (add text to photos)
Picmonkey.com (photo editor)
VSCO (adding photo filters)
Google Url Shortener (shorten website addresses)
Postano (curate content)
Repost (repost on Instagram)
Tagboard (search hashtags)
Thunderclap (message amplification tool)
Tweetdeck (Twitter management)
Visual.ly (create visual content)

CONTRIBUTORS

TODD ADKINS is the director of the leadership division of LifeWay Christian Resources. Prior to LifeWay, he served as an executive pastor at McLean Bible Church. Todd has a background in launching strategic initiatives and web-based leadership development, and is passionate about helping churches build a leadership pipeline and develop training pathways for every role in the church. He hosts the "5 Leadership Questions" podcast and tweets #Leadership incessantly at @ToddAdkins.

MATT BROWN is an evangelist, author, and founder of Think Eternity. He and his wife, Michelle, are impacting millions of people with the gospel each year online and through live events. They also minister to more than a million followers on social media daily. Connect with Matt: @evangelistmatt.

CLARK CAMPBELL, a committed learner, can be found chasing rabbits in social channels, articles, audio books, and conversations about digital opportunities in church communications. Clark is a ministry leader in a local church media ministry, an entrepreneur, and, most importantly, a husband and father. He started the social-web agency, SocialLion, Inc., in 2014 to amplify brands and events. Connect with Clark on Twitter: @BenjaminClark.

CHAD CANNON is the chief marketing officer for Michael Hyatt & Co., an online leadership development company that helps overwhelmed high achievers get the clarity, confidence, and tools they need to win at work and succeed at life. He was formerly the founder and CEO of Chadwick Cannon Agency, a full-service digital marketing firm dedicated to amplifying brands and ideas. Prior to that, he was vice president of marketing for

Thomas Nelson Publishers, now a division of HarperCollins. In his five years there, he led more than 225 book marketing campaigns, with sixteen titles reaching the New York Times Bestseller List. Chad lives in Nashville with his wife Julie, a talented photographer and writer. He's an enormous fan of the Chicago Cubs, Apple products, dogs, traveling, and good food.

DAVID DRURY became a church night janitor at age nineteen and since then has had similar jobs, such as church planter, executive pastor, and chief of staff of The Wesleyan Church. He is the author of nine books, including *Transforming Presence*, *Being Dad*, and *SoulShift*. Find him on DavidDrury.com or Twitter: @DavidDrury.

MARK FORRESTER is the senior director of public relations and communications for the General Council of the Assemblies of God (USA). He is charged with finding and telling the stories of the Assemblies of God across multiple teams and platforms. Along with Matt Brown and Haley Veturis, Mark organizes an annual summit for social media directors of Christian denominations and international faith-based nonprofit organizations. Mark is kept in line by his principal-wife, Janine, and his witty and rascally kids, Greyson and Charlotte. Connect with Mark on Twitter: @markgforrester.

DREW GNEISER is a storyteller and community builder who believes people are full of potential. In his career, Drew has done social media strategy, community management, and training with Fortune 100 companies, fast-growing nonprofits, small churches, and a monthly Meet-Up event for creative people. Connect with Drew on Twitter: @DrewGneiser.

AUSTIN GRAFF works in social media, marketing, and branding for *The Washington Post*. Previously, he led social media and influencer marketing for Honest Tea, America's number one organic bottled iced tea company. He also built a social media presence of five hundred thousand-plus fans across seven platforms for International Justice Mission, the largest nonprofit fighting human trafficking,. Growing up in Russia/Kazakhstan and attending boarding school in Germany, he now proudly calls Washington, DC, home (#DC4Life). He's also a superfan of the seventeen-year-old show *Survivor*. Connect with Austin on Twitter:@AustinKGraff.

SAM HOOVER is the social media manager for Compassion International, a child-development organization working to release children from poverty in Jesus' name. Sam lives in Colorado with his wife and three children. In a not-so-distant past, Sam's Facebook password used to be Boyz2Men4Eva! Connect with Sam on Twitter: @sam_hoover.

Formerly social media coordinator at Hillsong Church, JOSÉ HUERGO currently serves as worship brand manager for Hillsong Worship. Passionate about seeing churches grow their influence using social media, José believes the church has the potential to (and should) lead the way on all things digital. Born in California, José grew up in México and is now happy to call Australia home. Connect with him on Twitter: @JoseHuergo.

CARRIE KINTZ has honed her expertise and passion for communications and media over fifteen years in public relations and social media. She has consulted with start-ups and nonprofit organizations such as Focus on the Family and the Ethics and

Religious Liberty Commission. She is also a regular contributor at ChurchLeaders.com. Carrie shares her *Doctor Who* obsession and favorite book reviews on Twitter and Instagram. Connect with Carrie on Twitter: @CarrieKintz

BRIAN ORME is the senior content director at Open Doors USA and the founding editor of ChurchLeaders.com and Faithit. com. He oversees key publishing strategies, content marketing, story campaigns, and audience development. Brian is also a fish taco aficionado and enjoys long walks on the beach with his smartphone. Connect with Brian on Twitter:@mbrianorme.

ALLYSON SIWAJIAN is the digital engagement and communications liaison for The Foursquare Church denomination based in Los Angeles. When she's not tweeting to mobilize Christ-followers, Allyson taps social media to stay in touch with her fellow native Nevadans and to scope the latest *Star Wars* stories. Connect with Allyson on Twitter: @AllySiwaj.

NATE SMOYER is a marketing professional with expertise in the fields of digital marketing, social advertising, and influencer marketing. Outside his day job as owner of SmoyerProperties.com and realtor with Keller Williams Realty, Nate can be found reading about psychology while enjoying a fresh cup of coffee. He's an East Coast native struggling to live life at the joyous pace found in Bellingham, Washington. Connect with Nate on LinkedIn or his personal site: NateSmoyer.com.

HALEY VETURIS is the social media manager for Saddleback Church in Lake Forest, California. Haley cofounded the OC Social Media Summit, Social Ecclesia Conference, and was named one of *Christianity Today's* "Top 33 Under 33." Outside of ministry and social media, her passions include CrossFit, gourmet coffee, and college football (in that order). Connect with Haley on Twitter: @HaleyVeturis.

ACKNOWLEDGEMENTS

THIS PROJECT WOULD NOT HAVE BEEN POSSIBLE WITHOUT a remarkable level of interdenominational and interorganizational collaboration. My thanks to the many who contributed their precious time, knowledge, and skills to the insights found in *Trending Up*, and to each member of the #BestofSMS community. We're family!

Much gratitude goes to Matt Brown and Haley Veturis, who almost daily put up with my neurotic thoughts as we plan projects—like this book!—and our annual summits.

Lastly, I'm deeply indebted and grateful to the Assemblies of God for the opportunity to network with the great leaders represented in this book and for publishing these insights that will undoubtedly have an impact on church communications and churches nationwide.

— *Mark Forrester, General Editor*

FOR MORE INFORMATION

For more information about this
book and other valuable resources visit
www.TrendingUpBook.com.